HOLMIA
versus

Templ. S. Nicolai
Francisci
Templ. S. Ulrica
Arx Regia
Templ. S. Clara
Carlberg
Templ. S. Jacobi
SUBURBIUM
Solna
BOREALE

Ethel K. Smith Library

**Wingate University
Wingate, North Carolina 28174**

STOCKHOLM
Gullers/Ehrenmark

CONTENTS

INHALT

STOCKHOLM
Gullers/Ehrenmark

Photography: Peter Gullers
Björn Enström
Per-Erik Svedlund

Introduction: Torsten Ehrenmark
Design: Olle Eksell
Production: K.W. Gullers/Östen Matsson
Publisher: Gullers International ab

The park of Rålambshov and the West Bridge.

Der Rålambshovspark am Fuße der Westbrücke.

Birger Jarl—the city-builder.

Birger Jarl – Stockholms Gründer.

Jenny Lind—the Swedish Nightingale.

Jenny Lind – die schwedische Nachtigall.

Alfred Nobel—the man with the Prize.

Alfred Nobel – Stifter des Nobelpreises.

The Stockholmer

The Stockholmer is not very different from any other city-dweller in the world. In the old days more than 700 years ago he lived his life safe from enemies within his heavily guarded town wall. To him everything outside the wall was wilderness, filled with highwaymen, wild animals, dark forests and dangerous waters.
The Stockholmer of today probably lives in the suburbs of the city—of the 1.3 million inhabitants of Greater Stockholm only about 650 000 live in the centre.

Die Stockholmer

unterscheiden sich kaum von anderen typischen Städtern sonstwo auf der Welt. Früher lebte man wie anderswo im sicheren Schutze der ständig bewachten Stadtmauern. Draußen vor den Toren war Unsicherheit und Wildnis, mit Wegelagerern und wilden Tieren, unheimlichen Wäldern und gefahrvollen Wassern.
Der typische Stockholmer von heute lebt meistens in einem der Vororte – nur knapp die Hälfte der 1,3 Mio. Einwohner Groß-Stockholms haben ihren Wohnsitz in der eigentlichen Stadt.

August Strindberg—world-famous author.
Greta Garbo—the Legend.

August Strindberg – Autor mit Weltruf.
Greta Garbo – die Göttliche.

Ingrid Bergman—the Star.
Stieg Trenter—Stockholm Mystery Writer.

Ingrid Bergman – ein Weltstar.
Stieg Trenter – Kriminalschriftsteller.

Marcus Wallenberg—the Financier.

Marcus Wallenberg – Finanzmann.

Björn Borg—the World Champion.

Björn Borg – Weltchampion.

Carl XVI Gustaf—Monarch of Sweden.

Carl XVI. Gustaf – König von Schweden.

Carl Philip—prince

Victoria—princess.

Workmen—the men in the street.

Carl Philip – Prinz.

Victoria – Prinzessin.

Arbeiter – Mann auf der Straße.

A ford at the mouth of Lake Mälar, some islands surrounded by large forest tracts and glittering waters—that was the place chosen by Birger Jarl to build a fortress for the defence of Lake Mälar. The Mälar towns were seriously threatened by vandals from other parts and the Fortress of the Three Crowns on the island of Stadsholmen—the present Old Town of Stockholm—effectively guarded the prosperous Mälar towns and the fertile Mälar valley with its flourishing commerce. The town grew at amazing speed and construction was soon begun on the southern and northern islands. In the 17th century Stockholm was the capital at the centre of the Baltic Empire during Sweden's period as a major power. Present-day Stockholm has little in common with the Stockholm of the Middle Ages. The boulder ridge to the north has been flattened out by town planners and is less dramatic, to the benefit of motorists. Stockholm has spread out over the surrounding countryside and nowadays extends from

Nynäshamn in the south to Norrtälje in the north with commuter trains shuttling through the web of municipalities administered by the county council.

Naturally, all of Greater Stockholm does not look like a city. It consists of rural municipalities, small population centres, satellite towns, industrial areas alongside railway lines, colossal hypermarkets thrown up next to motorways and nowadays as accepted a part of the landscape as the surrounding lakes, streams and rocky outcrops.

Industry was born in the former tradesmen's slums in the various city boroughs and grew up in new districts in the south and on Kungsholmen. It is now to be found in modern complexes halfway out in the countryside and, as mentioned earlier, beside railways or next to harbours, like Scania Vabis in Södertälje or the multinational giant IBM which exports Swedish computer equipment to all parts of the world for many hundreds of millions of kronor. Or LM Ericsson which exports highly-advanced telecommunications systems to Saudi Arabia, Brazil and Great Britain. Or other worldwide corporations like Alfa Laval and Atlas Copco.

The plum in the cake or the pearl in the oyster, according to your

gastronomical preference, is nevertheless Stockholm itself. It is practically unchanged in the Old Town with its narrow medieval alleys and lovely 17th-century and 18th-century façades facing Skeppsbron, but completely rebuilt in the boroughs. Modern Stockholm nevertheless shares its magnificent situation on islands and skerries and beaches round Lake Mälar and the Baltic with the Stockholm of bygone days. Stand on the crown of Västerbron Bridge one sunny summer day and look out over Riddarfjärden towards the centre of Stockholm and the sight that greets your eyes is of such beauty that the worm's eye views over the Donau in Budapest or the Bosporus in Istanbul pale into insignificance. The background is dominated by the solid 17th-century massiveness of the

Wrangelska Palatset as a reminder of Sweden's period as a major power and on the left, as though floating on the water, Ragnar Östberg's graceful Town Hall with its three golden crowns surmounting the tower glittering in the sunshine. White sails flapping like butterflies over the blue water, sloops along the quays, sunbathers stretched out on the rocks of Långholmen and the lawns of Rålambshov Park—where else is there a city centre like this except perhaps in Rio de Janeiro?

Not to speak of all the public baths with saunas to suffer in or perhaps rather to enjoy before a dip in the heated pool, or the jogging paths in summer and the illuminated ski trails in winter. Stockholm has generous facilities for outdoor activities and recreation, even though comparisons with Siberia might spring to mind when approached in wintertime via the Arlanda tundra, lined by gloomy pine forests in the eternal half-light. But once in the city itself this first impression of banishment is soon forgotten as you get caught up in the festive generosity and bustling street life of the new city centre.

Modern Stockholm was born with violent birthpains during the 1950s, 1960s and 1970s. It was then that the underground railway was built, the city centre renewed and tunnels excavated under what was left of the boulder ridge. Approach roads from all directions were built at the same time, leading to this traffic complex that Stockholm comprises with all its islands, waterways and surprising rock outcrops, and above all the Essinge Highway, that sinuous concrete serpent from the southwest which gives the motorist a magnificent view of Stockholm if only he dared lift his eyes from the three highway lanes packed with vehicles travelling in urgent haste all around him.

How many Stockholmers are there in this city, the only one in Sweden with a million inhabitants?

Not many, if you are strict about the definition. A former colleague once traced his forefathers back to the 17th century—all in Stockholm. He considered himself to be one of a very select number of genuine Stockholmers, but even if you do not apply such strict criteria the genuine Stockholmer is still a minority in his own city. But they all come from the provinces and, in recent decades, from many countries in Europe as

well. In fact, every tenth Stockholmer is now an immigrant. Most are from Finland but many have also come from more faraway countries like Yugoslavia, Greece and Turkey. This out-of-the-way spot up in the North has become as cosmopolitan as Amsterdam or Trieste. I consider this to be an important phase in the development and maturity of Stockholm. These foreign invaders with their various cultures and customs are needed to make Stockholm the international rendezvous that a capital ought to be.

When the air grows warmer and summer is not far away the women of Stockholm blossom out in all their charm. Travellers from afar say with a sigh that "Women like this can't be seen anywhere else". And they are certainly attractive with their fresh complexions, springy step and summer dresses in bright colours. But then they are also daughters of the same city as Greta Garbo, Ingrid Bergman, Signe Hasso and Viveca Lindfors, to mention just a few who are

well-known from the world of the silver screen. Rumours that these attractive beings are also highly emancipated should be taken with a pinch of salt. They are also highly independent and therefore just as emancipated as they choose to be.

With greenery and water lying in wait behind practically every street corner, Stockholm is one of the world's most beautiful summer cities. As if that were not enough, an extravagant nature has on top of everything else strewn out 30 000 islands and skerries in the archipelago outside the capital where city dwellers spend their free time in the summer enjoying the sun, bathing, sailing and fishing. Many of these islands are large, wooded wildernesses, even hilly, while others have cultivated meadows or market gardens, the

products of which are destined for Stockholm. Far out in the archipelago the islands are smaller and more dramatic, barren and windswept with human habitation few and far between.

Stockholmers have enjoyed this archipelago as a summer paradise for more than 100 years. In the 1890s a fleet of white steamboats, leaving trails of smoke behind them like black candy floss, took hardworking husbands out to their families and summer houses on Saturday afternoons and brought them back to the city again on

Monday mornings. These journeys, on which a "steamboat steak" in the after-saloon was washed down with aquavit and beer followed by coffee and Swedish punch, were much longed-for and perhaps just as longed-for was the journey back to work on Monday morning and the whole week as a grass widower with all the more or less forbidden pleasures this made possible, an oft-recurring theme in the literature of that period. Nowadays there are only a few steamboats left and public transport is handled by faster vessels. Stockholm is sometimes called "the city on the water" and perhaps even more often "the Venice of the North". In spite of a conspicuous shortage of gondolas (and above all gondoleers), private small boats are so numerous that anyone thinking of acquiring a boat today must be prepared to wait five years for a mooring place even out in the suburbs, although Stockholm must have more miles of mooring berths than any other city of comparable size.

The wide locks between Stockholm's Ström and the sea in the east, and Riddarfjärden and Lake Mälar in the west, are as intensively trafficked on a Friday afternoon and Sunday evening as the German autobahns around Frankfurt with long queues of motorboats waiting their turn at the locks in Hammarbyleden and "Slussen".

In the summer, Stockholmers spend their leisuretime on the water and on the islands all round this capital so generously endowed by nature. It is said that the genuine Stockholmer does not feel at home anywhere but in his own city and its surroundings, and this is not hard to believe even though it must be admitted that during the long winters he will gladly spend a week or two in Majorca, Algarve, Rhodes or the Canary Islands. Stockholmers are also proud of

their city as Sweden's cultural centre. All the most important institutes of science and fine arts are located in Stockholm and their activities produce echoes throughout the world, whether they concern a film, an opera, an operation or photographing man's interior.

Birger Jarl's old pirate lock to Lake Mälar, half-way through history a wintry provincial hole in the outlying regions of Europe, which took the life of Europe's greatest philosopher Descartes, is now a handsome metropolis on a small scale.

And when foreign ships now come gliding up Strömmen it is not to plunder and despoil but so that tourists can enjoy themselves and go shopping in the glittering abundance of a scintillating Stockholm.

STOCKHOLM GESTERN UND HEUTE

Am Anfang war eine Furt an der Mündung des Mälar-Sees. Eine Handvoll kleiner Inseln, umgeben von gleißenden Wassern. Dichter Wald. Und natürlich Stadtgründer Birger Jarl, seines Zeichens Reichsverweser. Der wählte nämlich eben diesen strategischen Platz zur Befestigung der Mälar-Zufahrt. Recht so, denn in den Wirren jener Zeiten war Schwedens Kernland, die fruchtbare Mälar-Senke, einmal mehr von schweren Heimsuchungen durch fremde Heerscharen bedroht. Dort also, im Schutze der Burg „Drei Kronen", wo heute das königliche Schloß steht, entwickelte sich dann so allmählich das urkundlich erstmals 1252 erwähnte Stockholm.

Anfänglich beschränkt auf Stadsholmen, Riddarholmen und Helgeandsholmen – heute die Altstadt – wuchs Stockholm nicht nur schon bald auf die im Norden und Süden vorgelagerten anderen Inseln über, sondern auch an Bedeutung. Im 17. Jahrhundert mauserte es sich dann von der Hansestadt zur Reichshauptstadt. Zentral belegen in einem Schweden beidseitig der Ostsee, Gott hab es selig, denn das meiste sind wir wieder los.

Das Stockholm von heute hat jedoch nur noch wenig gemeinsam

mit dem von einst. Wo jetzt die City liegt, war früher Brunkeberg, eine gewaltige Moränenformation, inzwischen eingeebnet, autofreundlicher. Stockholm ist nicht nur über ihn hinweggekrochen, sondern auch weit über seine ländliche Umgebung. Lokalpatrioten rechnen Stockholm heute von Nynäshamn im Süden bis Norrtälje im Norden, d.h. alles, was man mit dem Pendelzug erreichen kann. Dieses Groß-Stockholm ist aber kein homogenes Stadtgebilde – Städte sind in Schweden schließlich sowieso abgeschafft. Immerhin: Schwedens größte Gemeinde in Schwedens größtem Ballungsgebiet. Mit einem Kranz von ländlichen Gemeinden, größeren und kleineren Ortschaften, dichter oder dünner besiedelt, selbständigen Satelliten... na halt eben doch Städten, wenn auch nur als Zugeständnis an den deutschen Sprachgebrauch. Überall in diesem Einzugsgebiet Riesen-Einkaufszentren an den Autobahnen – heute im Landschaftsbild genauso selbstverständlich wie alle Seen, Flüsse und Felsenhöhen, die wir übriggelassen haben.

Stockholms Industrie – hervorgegangen aus den ärmlichen Handwerkervierteln der damaligen Vorstadt und großgeworden in den Fabriken auf Söder und Kungsholmen – ist heute in modernen Komplexen weiter außerhalb angesiedelt. Oft entlang der Eisen-

1

bahn oder in Hafennähe wie Saab-Scania in Södertälje oder der multinationale Riese IBM, der allein von Schweden aus für viele Hunderte Millionen unserer Kronen exportiert. Oder LM Ericsson mit seinem weltweiten Export modernster Fernmeldeausrüstung. Oder Alfa-Laval und Atlas-Copco, um auch diese noch zu nennen. Das Schönste an diesem Groß-Stockholm aber ist Stockholm selbst. Fast unverändert in der Altstadt mit seinen mittelalterlichen Gassen und seiner berühmten Silhouette, fast völlig umgekrempelt im Bereich der heutigen Innenstadt. Geblieben ist jedoch seine einmalig schöne Lage auf unzähligen größeren und kleineren Inseln an der Schnittstelle zwischen Mälar- und Ostsee. Hoch oben auf der Westbrücke stehend, liegt einem dies Stockholm zu Füßen. Was ist dagegen schon die „Froschperspektive" über beispielsweise die Donau in Budapest oder den Bosporus in Istanbul? Gerade an einem sonnigen Spätnachmittag eröffnet sich von dort ein hinreißender Blick:

Wie aus dem Baukasten die Altstadt am Ende des Riddarfjärden. Mit dem wuchtigen Koloß des Wrangelschen Palastes, dessen Bauherr sich einst im Dreißigjährigen Krieg hervortat. Weiter links, gleichsam auf dem Wasser schwimmend, Stockholms Wahrzeichen Nr. 1, Ragnar Östbergs Stadthaus mit seinem charakteristischen Turm, den gleich drei Kronen zieren, weil die nun mal Schwedens Wappen sind. Und auf dem Riddarfjärden selbst ein Gewimmel von weißen Segeln. An den Kais reihenweise alte Schoner, deren neue Besitzer kaum ihren Geldbeutel schonen, um sie wieder seetüchtig zu machen. Und links und rechts am Fuße der Westbrücke scharen sich im Rålambshovspark und auf den Klippen Långholmens die Sonnenhungrigen, vereinzelt selbst zum

FKK. Und das mitten in der Stadt...
Überhaupt, badefreundlich ist Stockholm schon. Nicht nur am Riddarfjärden, der in letzter Zeit viel sauberer geworden ist. Unzählig fast die Strand-, Frei- und Hallenbäder, wo in der Sauna selbst Arbeitsscheue richtig ins Schwitzen kommen. Schweißgebadet auch die Jogger auf den vielen Trimm-Dich-Pfaden, die im Winter als Langlauf-Loipen dienen. Beleuchtet von Lampenketten, damit man sich nicht verfährt. Im Freizeitangebot mit sportlicher Note ist Stockholm eben groß. Auch mit einem Hauch von Abenteuer, denn noch gibt es Stellen, wo sich die Füchse gute Nacht sagen. Wer im Winter über Arlanda eingeschwebt ist, wird dies bestätigen können. Obwohl nur 40 Autominuten von Stockholm, glaubt man sich zuerst in Sibirien. Unendliche Tundra, ewige Halbdämmerung, die Schwermut der endlosen Nadelwälder. Erst mal in Stockholm, erholt man sich aber schnell vom ersten Eindruck der Verbannung. Reges Treiben in der Innenstadt, eine lebendige City, eine geschäftige Metropole.
Das moderne Stockholm erhielt sein heutiges Gesicht erst in den 50er bis 70er Jahren. Vielleicht keine ausgesprochene Schönheitsoperation, aber doch beeindruckend. In diesen Jahren wurden immerhin gewaltige Vorhaben rea-

lisiert: die gesamte U-Bahn, die bauliche Erneuerung der Innenstadt, die Autotunnels unter der City. Gleichzeitig entstanden immer neue Zufahrten in das wegen seiner vielen Inseln, Gewässer und steilen Höhen, verkehrstechnisch problematische Stockholm. So beispielsweise Essingeleden – Durchgangsstraße, Stadtautobahn und Teilstück der E4 im Südwesten Stockholms. Von seinen zahlreichen Betonviadukten riskierte schon so mancher Autofahrer den überwältigenden Blick, den man dort hat. Bis es krachte. Schöne Aussichten eben, aber bitte vorsichtig.
Stockholm ist Schwedens einzige Millionenstadt. Zugegeben: mit Vororten, aber wir Schweden sind nun mal großzügig. Stockholmer zu sein, ist schließlich was. Wer aber ist nun richtiger Stockholmer? Nicht jeder daselbst geborene kann eine Ahnentafel vorzeigen, die vielleicht bis ins 17. Jahrhundert zurückreicht und ihn als Ur-Stockholmer ausweist. Selbst wenn man nicht so weit geht, eins ist klar: echte Stockholmer sind in

ihrer Stadt eine Minderheit. Die meisten sind Zugezogene, Landflüchtige aus der Provinz, Wahl-Stockholmer. In den letzten Jahrzehnten verstärkt durch ein erhebliches Kontingent an Einwanderern aus dem Ausland. In erster Linie aus Finnland, aber auch Jugoslawien, Griechenland und der Türkei. Mittlerweile ist nun schon jeder zehnte Stockholmer das, was wir nicht etwa Gastarbeiter, sondern Einwanderer nennen. Auch da sind wir großzügig, wir beteiligen sie sogar an der Wahl unserer Kommunalpolitiker. Und das wiederum ist beispielhaft. Stockholm hat jedenfalls durch eben diese Einwanderer gewonnen, ist heute weltstädtischer, nicht nur ,,Schwedens größte Hauptstadt der Welt'', wie früher gewitzelt wurde.

Wenn der lange Winter dem kurzen, aber desto intensiveren Frühling weicht, die linden Lüfte erwachen, blüht Stockholm so richtig auf. Und die Stockholmerin. Mit ihrem gewissen Etwas, das selbst den zurückhaltendsten Globetrotter ins Schwärmen verfallen

läßt. Und das oft ohne Kriegsbemalung. Durch einfache Natürlichkeit, ihren unnachahmlichen Gang, ihr Selbstbewußtsein. Das macht sie so attraktiv wie schon Greta Garbo und Ingrid Bergman, zwei Töchter Stockholms, welche die Stockholmerin zumindest im Film weltbekannt gemacht haben. Ins Reich der Fabel gehört dagegen, daß sie besonders freizügig sei. Nur selbständiger vielleicht. So selbständig jedenfalls, daß schon so manchem das Gefühl der eigenen Unwiderstehlichkeit gründlich vergangen ist.

Mit Grünflächen und Gewässern hinter fast jeder Ecke ist Stockholm zur Sommerszeit eine der schönsten Städte der Welt. Als ob dies allein nicht schon reichen würde, hat Mutter Natur den Küstenstreifen vor der Stadt verschwenderisch mit über 30000 Inseln und Inselchen angereichert, den sogenannten Schären. Als standesbewußter Stockholmer holt man sich dort die notwendige Sommerfrische. Beim Segeln, Fischen, Baden oder auch nur einfach Sonnen. Viele dieser Inseln sind reinste Wildnis, felsig und voller Dickicht. Andere dagegen sind idyllisches Ackerland, in schwielig fester Hand von Gartenbauern, die Stockholm mit Vitaminen versorgen. Weiter draußen werden die Inseln immer spärlicher, kärger und unwirtlicher, windgepeitschter.

Als Sommerparadies der Stockholmer haben die Schären lange Tradition. Ganze Flotten weißer Dampfschiffe mit ihrem schwarzen Wald von Rauchfahnen um 1890. Jeden Samstagmittag brachten sie die illustre Schar derzeitiger Familienversorger zum gemeinsamen Wochenende mit den wartenden Lieben im Sommerhäuschen. Damals noch eine richtige Reise, aber heißersehnt. Schon wegen des sogenannten Dampfer-Beefsteaks mit Bratkartoffeln, Bier und Aquavit, Kaffee und Schwedenpunsch im Achtersalon. Nicht minder ersehnt die Rückfahrt am Montagmorgen, aber weniger der Schaffensfreude wegen. Was lockte, war vielmehr das Strohwitwerdasein mit all seinen mehr oder weniger verbotenen Freuden. So zumindest schildert es die Literatur jener Zeit. Die Dampfer von

damals sind inzwischen meist verschrottet und ersetzt durch schnelle Motorschiffe. Der Wochenendverkehr ist heute aber mindestens noch genauso rege wie einst.

Unsere Fremdenverkehrswerbung rühmt Stockholm als ,,Stadt auf dem Wasser''. Lassen wir's da hingestellt. Macht sich schließlich gut so. Noch besser macht sich vielleicht ,,Venedig des Nordens'', was aber auch nur bedingt stimmt. Was fehlt, sind erstens die Gondeln und zweitens die Gondolieri. Dafür haben wir umso mehr lieblich tuckernde und gluckernde Motor- und Segelboote. Die Stockholmer haben sich mittlerweile so viele Boote angeschaffte, daß die Wartezeit für freie Liegeplätze bis zu fünf Jahren beträgt. Selbst in den Vororten, und obwohl Stockholm sicherlich mehr Kai-km zu bieten hat als manch andere Stadt. Auf den Gewässern rund um und in Stockholm herrscht freitags- und sonntagsabends jedenfalls ein unbeschreibliches Gedränge. Hier hat das Fremdenverkehrsamt mal recht –

The City Hall that 'floats on the water'.

Stadshuset, Stockholms Wahrzeichen
Nr. 1.

3

eine ganze Stadt „auf dem Wasser". An den beiden Schleusen zwischen Mälar- und Ostsee bilden sich dann Staus wie auf der Autobahn. Auch das eine Sehenswürdigkeit.

Das von der Natur so großzügig ausgestattete Stockholm ist seinen Einwohnern im Sommer verlockend genug. Es wird sogar behauptet, daß ein rechter Stockholmer sich nur eben dort wohlfühle und Urlaubsreisen höchstens in die nähere Umgebung mache. Da ist schon was dran, obwohl nur im Sommer. Wenn der lange Winter dräut, zieht es nämlich oft selbst die eingefleischtesten Stockholmer gen Süden. Zumindest für ein paar Wochen. Bis das Heimweh sie zurücktreibt von Mallorca, Rhodos oder den Kanarischen Inseln, die allen Eingemeindungsversuchen bisher noch widerstanden haben.

Stolz sind die Stockholmer aber auch darauf, daß ihre Stadt gleichzeitig das Zentrum des schwedischen Kulturlebens darstellt. Die Wissenschaften und die schönen Künste haben dort nämlich seit alters her ihre wichtigsten Institutionen. So manches hat inzwischen Weltruf oder zumindest weltweit Aufsehen erregt. Ob Filmschaffen, Operninszenierungen, Chirurgie oder Lennart Nilssons Farbbilder aus dem menschlichen Innenleben – in Stockholm werden Geistesleistungen eben nicht nur durch noble Preise gewürdigt, sondern auch selbst vollbracht.

Stockholm – ursprünglich Verteidigungsanlage gegen Seeräuberhorden, dann lange Zeit ein winterkaltes Provinznest am Rande der Zivilisation, das einen so großen Denker wie Descartes geradezu umbringen mußte, und auch tat – ist heute eine elegante Weltstadt im Kleinformat. Wenn heute fremde Schiffe in den Meeresarm nach Stockholm einfahren, kommen sie nicht wie einst zum Plündern und Brandschatzen. Heute bringen sie eine Touristeninvasion zum friedlichen Shopping, Souvenirjäger und aufgeklärte Verbraucher, Bildungsreisende und Amüsierwillige. Stockholm empfängt sie alle mit offenen Armen, schließt sie ans Herz und läßt sie nicht wieder los.

The Old Town—mysterious, fascinating...

Die Altstadt – lebendiges Museum für Bau-
kunst.

Mårten Trotzig's Alley, only three feet wide at its narrowest point.

Mårten Trotzigs gränd – mit 90 cm an der schmalsten Stelle Stockholms engste Gasse.

The Old Town

It was called *"the Lock to the lake Mälaren"*, the city that was built by the great Birger Jarl in the 13th century.
A fortress to guard the rich inland counties, a church, a market place, and a huge town wall, all on one small island: that was Stockholm in 1250.
In 1697 disaster struck: the Fortress of the Three Crowns burned down—but the present Palace was built, happily, on the same site. And Stockholm spread outside its wall and spilled over onto the other islands surrounding it.
Modern Stockholm had been born.

Die Altstadt

"Schlüssel zum Mälar-See" ist Stockholms Beiname aus der Zeit seiner Gründung durch Reichsverweser Birger Jarl im frühen 13. Jahrhundert.
Eine Burg, eine Kirche, ein Marktplatz, einer mächtigen Stadtmauer, alles noch auf einer einzigen kleinen Insel: das war Stockholm um 1250.
1697 die Katastrophe: die Burg „Drei Kronen" brannte vollständig nieder. An gleicher Stelle wurde später dann das heutige Schloß erbaut. Und Stockholm wuchs über seine Mauern hinaus auch auf die angrenzenden Inseln über.
Für Stockholm hatte damit die Neuzeit begonnen.

Perhaps the best-known of all Old Town restaurants: Gyldene Freden, the Golden Peace. Dates back to the 18th century.

„Gyldene Freden" oder „Zum goldenen Frieden" – eine Perle unter den Restaurants der Altstadt, mit Tradition bis ins 18. Jahrhundert.

Towers of Stockholm.

Von Türmen überragt: die Altstadt.

The small-town atmosphere of the Old Town.

Altstadt-Idylle.

One of the main tourist attractions: The changing of the guard at the Palace.

Wachablösung am Königlichen Schloß wie hier zu Pferde – eine der größten Touristenattraktionen.

Where would you expect quaint old shop-signs if not in the Old Town?

Ladenschilder von anno dazumal, natürlich in der Altstadt.

The window of a thousand small things...

Trödlerladen, wie ihn nur die Altstadt bietet.

MÅNGA OLIKA
ANTECKNINGS
BÖCKER
FRÅN 3~

EN DOCKA MED
TRE ANSIKTEN
50~

In the northern part of the city you can skate and ski right outside your apartment building.

Gärdet im Stockholmer Norden – Möglichkeiten zum Ski- und Schlittschuhlaufen direkt vor der Haustür.

The Milles sculpture garden—a memorial over one of the greatest Swedish artists, Carl Milles.

Millesgården – dem großen schwedischen Bildhauer Carl Milles gewidmetes Museum.

The Swedish Museum of Natural History.

Stockholm's House of Culture.

Naturhistorisches Museum.

Stockholms Kulturhaus.

The National Museum of Science and Technology.

Technisches Museum und Telemuseum.

Museums

There are 52 museums to choose from, ranging from Near and Far Eastern Antiquities and the magnificent National Museum of Fine Arts to the Wasa Dockyard—Wasa, the ill-fated ship that sank on her maiden voyage in 1628 and was raised 333 years later.
For those interested in beautiful old buildings and history the 18th century palace of Gustav III at Haga is a must—as well as the Drottningholm Theatre, the 18th-century theatre which has remained untouched for the last two centuries.

Museen

Was immer interessieren mag, Stockholm hat bestimmt ein entsprechendes Museum. Genauer gesagt 52, von Museen für ägyptische und ostasiatische Frühgeschichte über das Nationalmuseum mit seiner stattlichen Kunstsammlung bis hin zur ,,Wasa'', dem 1628 auf seiner Jungfernfahrt gesunkenen Regalschiff, das 333 Jahre später geborgen und in einem eigenen Museum untergebracht wurde.
Für architekturhistorisch Interessierte ist das unter Gustav III. im 18. Jahrhundert erbaute Sommerschloß Haga ein Muß – genauso wie das Drottningholmer Schloßtheater, unverändert seit seiner Erbauung im 18. Jahrhundert.

The Modern Museum at Skeppsholmen fea-
tures a permanent exhibition of Swedish
and international art from this century.

Das Museum für Moderne Kunst auf
Skeppsholmen beherbergt eine ständige
Ausstellung internationaler zeitgenössi-
scher Kunst.

Wasa, the King's ship, the unfortunate.
Launched in 1628 she sank on her maiden
voyage, was salvaged 333 years later. Now
on display at Djurgården.

Die unglückliche „Wasa" – 1628 zu Wasser
gelassen und auf der Jungfernfahrt gesun-
ken, 333 Jahre später geborgen und jetzt auf
Djurgården zu besichtigen.

Industry

Stockholm is the world's cleanest
industrial city. The townscape has
no belching chimneys and noisy
factories. While Swedish industry
is chiefly characterized by heavy
raw materials processing, Stockholm is the centre of new engineering fields such as energy
(Studsvik AB), advanced commun-
ications (L M Ericsson),
pharmaceuticals for welfare dis-
eases (Astra) or microelectronics
(ASEA-Hafo).
Stockholm is a decentralized industrial city which has no exploit-
ed industrial areas.

Industrie

Ohne die sonst üblichen qualmen-
den Schornsteine und lärmenden
Fabriken ist Stockholm als Indu-
striestadt eine der saubersten der
Welt.
Während für Schweden sonst mehr
die auf heimischen Rohstoffen ba-
sierende Schwerindustrie typisch
ist, wird Stockholms Industrie
durch modernste Technologie ge-
prägt. Beispielsweise in den Berei-
chen Energietechnik (Studsvik
AB), Fernmeldetechnik (L.M.
Ericsson), Pharmakologie (Astra)
oder Mikroelektronik (ASEA-
Hafo).
Stockholm hat seine Industrie heute mehr oder weniger ausgesiedelt.

Rock handling is a field of engineering in which Sweden leads the world through Atlas Copco. Equipment is tested in a laboratory mine about 10 km from the Royal Palace.

Weltmeister im Gesteinsbohren: Atlas Copco mit seinem eigenen Labor-Bergwerk 10 km vom Stockholmer Schloß.

At all events two towns of Stockholm's
dimensions ca be supported with power by
Forsmark's nuclear power station. Nuclear
power plants delivered ASEA-Atom.

Forsmarks Kernkraftstation kann
mindestens zwei Städte von Stockholms
Größe mit Elektrizität versorgen. Die
Kernkraftanlagen hat ASEA-Atom
geliefert.

Lilla Essingen, the head quarter of the well-known Electrolux concern.

Lilla Essingen, das Hauptbüro des wohlbekamten Konzerns Electrolux.

The world's leading manufacturer of computers, IBM, is expanding in Stockholm. Several of the corporation's most modern units are manufactured in Stockholm for the European market.

IBM investiert weiter in Stockholm, wo schon heute ein Großteil seiner modernsten Anlagen für Export nach ganz Europa gebaut wird.

Parks

Stockholm is a green city, about a third of the total area consists of parks. The long shores of the lake invite the Stockholmer to stroll on 170 miles of shaded paths—and if you get tired there are 8 000 park benches to choose from ...
Swedes love animals; the city of Stockholm regularly feeds thousands of birds and also sees to it that there is no housing shortage for the song-birds—there are 9 000 nesting boxes in the parks.
Children are, of course, also taken care of; 5 million children attend 'park activities'.

Parks

Stockholm ist wahrlich eine grüne Stadt. Nahezu ein Drittel seiner Gesamtfläche entfallen auf Parkanlagen. Mit schattigen Uferpromenaden von fast 275 km Gesamtlänge. Und über 8000 Parkbänken für müde Wanderer.
Im tierliebenden Stockholm sorgt man sich besonders um unsere gefiederten Freunde. Mit eigens eingerichteten Futterplätzen für überwinternde Seevögel und über 9000 Nistkästen in den Parks.
Für Kinder ist natürlich nicht weniger gesorgt: die von der Stadtverwaltung auf Spielplätzen usw. veranstalteten Freizeitaktivitäten locken alljährlich rund 5 Millionen junge Besucher.

Haga, large park north of the city centre, is a favourite spot for Stockholmers. Here a summer-festival in front of the copper tents built in the 18th century.

In summer the city offers Stockholmers free entertainment in parks and squares. Here theatre in the market-place of the Old Town.

Haga – ausgedehnter Park im Norden der Stadt, beliebtes Ausflugsziel der Stockholmer. Hier ein sommerliches Festival vor dem sogenannten Kupferzelt aus dem 18. Jahrhundert.

Im Sommer sorgt die Stadtverwaltung für kostenlose Unterhaltung in Parks und auf Plätzen wie hier in der Altstadt mit einer Theateraufführung.

The King's Garden, the fountain of Molin,
popular meeting-place.

Kungsträdgården mit Molins Fontäne –
früher königlicher Garten, heute Treffpunkt
der Stockholmer.

Playground for children by the fountain of
Blom.

Kühlung in Stadt-Gartenbaumeister Holger
Bloms Springbrunnen.

5

King's Garden where the gigantic chess-board draws scores of players and spectators.

Großschachmeisterturnier im Kungsträdgården.

How many large cities can boast of water clear enough to swim in?

Stockholms saubere Gewässer ermöglichen gefahrloses Baden selbst mitten in der Stadt.

Winter in Stockholm.

Winterliches Stockholm.

Sweeping highways criss-cross the landscape in the south of Stockholm.

Verkehrsknotenpunkt Årsta im südlichen
Stockholm.

Traffic

Like all large cities Stockholm is
waging a losing battle against its
traffic. The number of cars is
steadily increasing; in 1965 there
were 320 000 private cars in greater Stockholm—in 1977 the number
had risen to 405 000. Whereas bicycles are on the decrease, from
9 000 in 1965 to 5 000 in 1977.
It is, of course, dangerous to ride a
bicycle in the city although the Bicycle Association is doing its ut-
most to get Stockholmers back on
their bikes: excellent exercise, no
exhaust fumes!

Verkehr

Wie alle Großstädte kämpft auch
Stockholm mit seinem ständig
wachsenden Verkehr. Der Auto-
vormarsch scheint unaufhaltbar.
Waren 1965 in Groß-Stockholm
noch 320 000 PKWs zugelassen,
stieg ihre Zahl bis 1977 auf ganze
405 000. Die Zahl der Fahrräder
dagegen ist im gleichen Zeitraum
von 9000 auf 5000 zurückgegan-
gen.
Radfahrer leben freilich immer
noch gefährlich im Stadtverkehr,
wenn auch ihre rührigen Interes-
senverbände keine propagandisti-
schen Mühen scheuen, die Stockholmer wieder fürs Zweirad zu be-
geistern. Strampeln ist gesund und
verpestet vor allem keine Luft!

The number of bicycles in the city is decreasing in spite of publicity campaigns from the cyclists themselves.

Trotz starker Zweiradpropaganda immer weniger Drahtesel.

The main artery of Stockholm, the Essinge highway, takes a load off the congested city-streets.

Stockholms Stadtautobahn ,,Essingeleden'' entlastet die alten Zubringerstraßen.

The suburbanite's curse: congested highways to and from work.

But even on the fast commuter-trains the waiting can be long...

A most pleasant way of getting to work every day—the Archipelago steamers.

Kilometerlange Verkehrsstaus auf dem Wege von und zur Arbeit – Alptraum jedes Vorortpendlers...

... doch auch beim Pendelzug heißt's Schlangestehen.

Privilegiert dagegen die Pendler aus den Schären: mit Volldampf zur Arbeit.

4

Suburbs

The city of Stockholm is spreading—new suburbs grow up where 20 years ago there were only fields and woods. Many of these new suburbs have become models attracting international interest. Now the trend is changing, Swedes do not really want to live in high-rise buildings. New suburbs are experimenting with large areas of chain houses where each family has its own small garden. Service-centres, shops and offices make these new suburbs miniature cities in themselves instead of the dormitory towns of the last few decades.

Vororte

Das Stadtgebiet von Stockholm dehnt sich ständig weiter aus. Wo noch vor 20 Jahren weit und breit nur Wald und Felder, stehen heute moderne Vororte – vielfach Vorbilder auch für andere Weltstädte. Inzwischen bahnt sich ein anderer Trend an, denn immer weniger Schweden wollen in Hochhäusern wohnen. Bei neuen Vororten experimentiert man deshalb heute mit Reihen- und Kettenhaussiedlungen, wo jede Familie einen eigenen kleinen Garten hat.

The underground station—the teenage meeting-place.

Rotebro—an old suburb under development.

U-Bahnhof – Treffpunkt der Stadtjugend.

Rotebro – älterer Vorort in Weiterentwicklung.

Akalla—one of the newest suburbs.

Akalla, einer von Stockholms neuesten
Vororten.

The hospital of Danderyd, one of the largest and most modern in Stockholm with 1 268 beds.

The hospital of Sollentuna, one of the newest.

Krankenhaus Danderyd – mit 1268 Betten eines der größten und modernsten Stockholms.

Das neue Krankenhaus im Vorort Sollentuna.

Large-scale expansion of medical care facilities outside hospitals is in progress. The expansion programme includes a number of new medical care centres like this one in Matteus parish.

Die medizinische Betreuung erfolgt nicht nur in Krankenhäusern. Überall werden neue Kapazitäten ausgebaut wie hier die Mathäus-Gemeinde.

Health care

Through compulsory health insurance (subsidized by taxes) everybody gets medical care practically free, including specialist care and medicines.
There are 24 000 hospital beds in Stockholm—and they are in constant use; in 1977 260 000 patients were admitted into hospital.
One item of interest: in the Serafimer Hospital in Stockholm, the oldest in the city, one Catholic bed, paid for by the Catholic community in Stockholm, is always ready for a Catholic, in Protestant Sweden.

Gesundheitswesen

Durch die obligatorische Krankenversicherung – Beitragseinziehung per Steuer – ist die ärztliche Versorgung für jedermann praktisch kostenlos, einschließlich Spezialistenbetreuung und Arzneimittel.
Stockholm verfügt über 24 000 Krankenhausbetten – so gut wie ständig belegt, denn allein 1977 wurden 260 000 Patienten eingewiesen.
Erwähnenswert am Rande: im Serafimer-Lazarett, Stockholms ältestem Krankenhaus, steht für Katholiken stets ein Freibett, bezahlt von der dortigen katholischen Gemeinde im sonst streng protestantischen Schweden.

Lesson at the Dental College, Stockholm.

Mammography—X-raying for cancer of the breast.

Computerized tomography—complicated new X-ray-method.

Übungsbetrieb an der Hochschule für Zahnmedizin.

Mammographie – Röntgenuntersuchung zur Vorbeugung von Brustkrebs.

Computergesteuerte Tomographie – neuentwickeltes Röntgenverfahren.

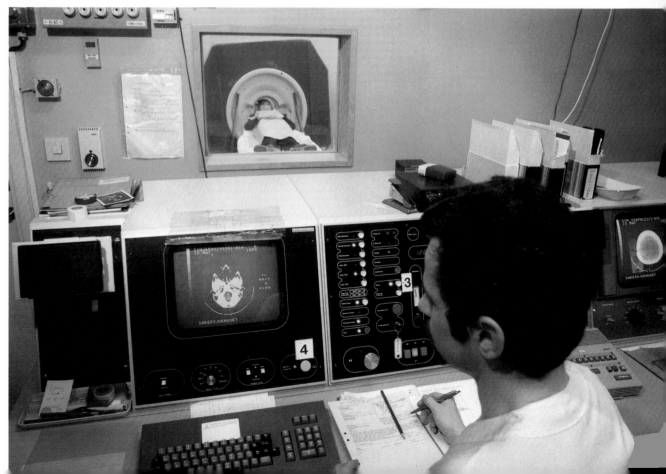

5

At the Karolinska Institute, brain tumours
are removed surgically without opening the
skull using a unique radiation knife—one of
only two in the world.

Operative Entfernung von Gehirntumoren
mit dem Strahlenskalpell im Karolinska In-
stitutet, wo eine der beiden einzigen auf der
Welt existierenden Anlagen dieser Art
steht.

Research

Stockholm is northern Europe's
cradle of research and an important international centre for development work.
Basic research is carried out pri-
marily at the University and in colleges. Inventions with Stockholm
as their birthplace are legion and
they span everything from the
principle of the refrigerator (Pla-
ten-Munters) to the latest discov-
eries in cancer research (Karolinska).
What only Stockholm has are aca-
demies—eight of them. Most are
known for awarding Nobel prizes.

Forschung

Stockholm ist ganz Skandinaviens
Zentrum für Forschungs- und
Entwicklungsarbeit, international
mit gutem Ruf.
Reine Grundlagenforschung be-
treiben vor allem die Universitäten
und Hochschulen.
Erfindungen sind in Stockholm
unzählige entstanden. Vom Prinzip
des Kühlschranks (Platen-Mun-
ters) bis hin zu Innovationen der
Krebsforschung (Karolinska Insti-
tutet).
An altehrwürdigen Akademien hat
Stockholm ganze acht, die meisten
bekannt durch die Nobelpreise.

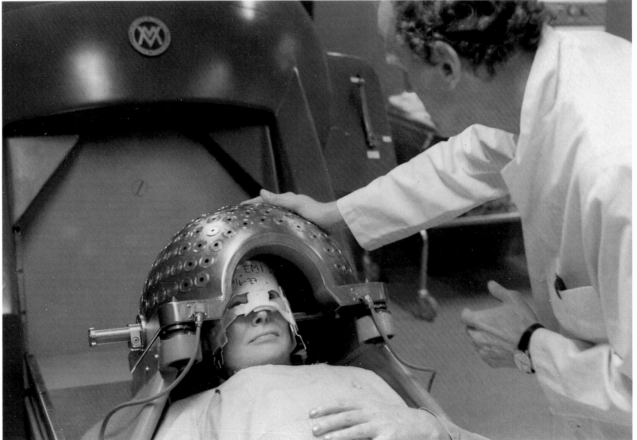

The Arrhenius laboratory is a centre of chemical and biological research. The latest line of research concerns bio-energy engineering.

Im Arrheniuslaboratorium, einem weltbekannten Zentrum für chemische und biologische Forschung, diskutiert man einen neuen Forschungszweig: Biotechnik.

Thought is about the only thing he hasn't photographed so far—that is what they sometimes say about world-famous photographer Lennart Nilsson.

,,Das einzige, was er noch nicht fotografiert hat, sind Gedanken,'' sagt man vom weltberühmten Lennart Nilsson.

The deaf cannot hear but they can see on the screen what is being said and learn to speak with the computer system at the Royal Institute of Technology.

Per Bildschirm lernen Taube in der Königlichen Technischen Hochschule mit dem Computer sprechen.

Stockholm is perhaps best known
throughout the world for the Nobel banquet
in December every year. Gyllene Salen,
Town Hall.

Festbankett im Stadshuset nach der alljährlich im Dezember stattfindenden Nobel-
preisverleihung.

In the centre of public interest for several
years, Queen Silvia is the most popular
guest.

Königin Silvia – als Ehrengast ständig im
Blickpunkt der Feierlichkeiten.

The longest night of the year—Midsummer Eve—is celebrated all over Sweden at the end of June.

Mittsommer, das Fest der Sommersonnenwende, wird Ende Juni in ganz Schweden gefeiert.

Walpurgis night: All over Sweden bonfires greet spring.

Walpurgisnacht am Vorabend des 1. Mai – überall Freudenfeuer als Willkommensgruß an den Frühling.

Not a single polar bear in the streets of Stockholm—but here they are, at Skansen!

Die einzigen Eisbären in Stockholm: die von Skansen.

Skansen

Skansen—a large open-air museum close to the centre of town—is a must for anybody interested in Swedish culture through the ages. To Skansen have been moved old buildings from all over the country, reerected here as a reminder of our cultural heritage. The "kåta" of the Lapp, the shielding from Dalecarlia, the lovely old whitewashed cottage from the south of Sweden.
A small zoo with Swedish animals completes this miniature Sweden.

Skansen

Ganz in Zentrumnähe liegt das Freilichtmuseum Skansen – ein Miniaturschweden quer durch die gesamte Kulturgeschichte. Mit einer typischen Lappenbehausung, Almhütten aus Dalarna und neben vielen weiteren Gehöften aus allen Teilen Schwedens schließlich ein weißgekalkter, strohdachbedeckter Prachthof aus Schonen.
Mit seinen Tiergehegen ist Skansen gleichzeitig auch ein kleiner Zoo, sogar mit Aquarium.

Skogaholm, 18th century country manor house.

Herrensitz von Skogaholm aus dem 18. Jahrhundert.

Ships that meet... The Viking-line runs almost daily to Finland.

Reger Verkehr der Fährschiffe zwischen Stockholm und Finnland.

Harbours

Stockholm has nine harbours, mainly on the Baltic side of the city, with 21 miles of quay. Most of these are regular freight harbours. The best known to Stockholmers are the two oldest ones in the Old Town although these have lost the importance they once had in the Middle Ages. Some of the Finland ferries dock here as well as cruise-liners on short—but spectacular—visits to Stockholm.

Häfen

Stockholm hat insgesamt gleich neun Häfen mit gut 34 km Kai. Die meisten liegen ostseewärts und sind reine Umschlaghäfen.
Am vertrautesten sind den Stockholmern die beiden ältesten in der Altstadt. Ihre Bedeutung ist inzwischen jedoch dahin, denn heute legen dort nur noch ein paar Finnland-Fähren an. Und Kreuzfahrtschiffe, die in Stockholm gern eine Stippvisite machen.

The Stockholm container terminal—best
equipped on the east coast.

Stockholms Containerterminal – der modernste Hafen an der schwedischen Ost-
küste.

Oil harbour.

Tankerhafen vor der Stadt.

The Östermalm food market, also a popular
luncheon-place, for seafood-lovers.

Markthalle Östermalm – Paradies für Fein-
schmecker, wo jeden Mittag die Fisch-
freunde tafeln.

Lars Trollberg's sculptures dance in the
court yard of the Trygg-Hansa insurance-
company building.

,,Noahs Tanz'', Plastik von Lars Trollberg
auf dem Hof der Hauptverwaltung der Ver-
sicherungsgesellschaft Trygg-Hansa.

The Berwald Hall, newest music studio of
the Swedish Broadcasting Corp., designed
by architect Erik Ahnborg.

Die Berwald-Halle – von Architekt Erik
Ahnborg entworfenes neues Musikstudio
des schwedischen Rundfunks.

Even the underground has a heaven...

Kunsthimmel in der Stockholmer U-Bahn.

Art in children's playground in the south of Stockholm.

Von Künstlern entworfener Kinderspielplatz im Süden Stockholms.

Art

Stockholm is not only a lovely city with its waters, parks and old buildings—Stockholm is also a city of art. Wherever you go you find works of art, mainly sculptures and murals, by many of Sweden's most famous artists.
The city also organizes temporary exhibitions in parks and in the main squares of the city.
The Stockholm underground has been called "the longest art gallery in Sweden"—35 underground stations have been decorated by well-known Swedish artists.

Kunst

Stockholm ist mit seinen Gewässern, Parks und alten Gebäuden nicht nur eine schöne Stadt, sondern auch eine Stadt der schönen Künste. Überall stößt man auf Kunstwerke wie Plastiken und Wandgemälde der bedeutendsten Künstler Schwedens.
Die Stadt veranstaltet darüberhinaus in Parks, auf Plätzen usw. eine Vielzahl von zeitweiligen Ausstellungen die immer wieder starken Anklang finden.
,,Schwedens längste Kunstgalerie'' ist zweifellos die Stockholmer U-Bahn. Ganze 35 U-Bahnhöfe wurden inzwischen von zeitgenössischen schwedischen Künstlern gestaltet.

Northern Lights symbolised by this glass obelisk in the centre of the city. Artist Edvin Öhrström used 80 000 pieces of glass in construction.

,,Aurora Borealis'' nennt Edvin Öhrström seinen das Nordlicht verkörpernden Glasobelisken im Stadtzentrum, den er aus über 80 000 Glasstücken gefertigt hat.

The Kaknäs' television tower, 508 feet, tallest building in Scandinavia.

Der Kaknästurm – einer der beiden Fernsehtürme Stockholms, mit 155 Metern Skandinaviens höchstes Bauwerk.

7

Sports

The Stockholmer is discovering physical fitness. In 1891 the Stockholm Sports Association was founded with 8 clubs; today, 80 years later, there are 2 092 clubs with 607 434 members!
City-people begin to realize that they feel better, and live longer, with exercise. And the Stockholmer can choose from 54 different organized sporting activities, from badminton to skin-diving. Continuous publicity through news media is making physical fitness a national movement.

Sport

Die Stockholmer sind sportfreudige Leute. Der 1891 von 8 Vereinen gegründete Stockholmer Sportverband umfaßt heute, 80 Jahre später, ganze 2092 Vereine mit insgesamt 607 434 Mitgliedern. Die Stadtbewohner scheinen entdeckt zu haben, daß sportliche Betätigung das körperliche Wohlbefinden und die Lebenserwartung erhöht. Wer will, kann zwischen 54 Sportarten wählen, vom Badminton bis hin zum Sporttauchen. In den Massenmedien wird darüberhinaus ständig für sportliche Fitneß geworben, so daß man heute von einer nationalen Trimm-Dich-Bewegung sprechen kann.

The Lidingö Race—yearly contest with
8 000 participants.

Lidingö-Lauf – traditioneller Volkslauf mit
alljährlich über 8000 Teilnehmern.

Youth is coming on strong in all kinds of
sports, thousands take part regularly in the
most varied sports activities.
The Stockholm football stadium in Solna:
Soccer fans.

Stockholms Jugend drängt zum Sport, wo
sie sich zu Tausenden in den unterschied-
lichsten Sportarten messen.

The Stockholm fotball stadium at Solna:
Soccer fans.

Råsunda – Stockholms Fußballstadion, wo
Brasilien 1958 Weltmeister wurde.

The Vanadis pool, one of 30 favourite
summer-spots for Stockholmers.

Vanadisbadet – eins der 30 Stockholmer
Freibäder mit temperiertem Becken.

The Långholmen canal.

Der Kanal von Långholmen – romantischer
Wasserweg in die Freizeit.

Sandhamn—the Mecca of yachtsmen.

Sandhamn – das Mekka der Stockholmer
Segler.

Utö—the vacation-paradise of Stockholmers.

Utö – Urlaubsparadies der Stockholmer.

Utö: Sweden at its best—old cottages from
the 18th century.

Utö – Schweden von seiner besten Seite.
Tagelöhnerbehausungen aus dem 18. Jahrhundert.

8

Archipelago

The Stockholm archipelago is
unique in the world. With 30 000
islands and a total area of about
126 square miles of ever-changing
scenery, from the softly wooded
islands near the mainland to the
stark cliffs of the outer archipelago.
For those who do not own a boat
or house of their own on one of the
islands the Stockholm Archipelago
Foundation has established the
'Utö project'. On the island of Utö
there is every facility for Stockholmers: a hotel, small apart-
ments, service-centre, boats and
bikes for rent.

Schären

Ohne Gegenstück sonstwo auf der
Welt sind die Stockholmer Schären. Mit über 30 000 Inseln und
einer Gesamtfläche von rund 6000
km². Mit Wald bestandene große
Inseln in Festlandnähe und kleine,
karge Klippen zur offenen See hin.
Für alle, die kein eigenes Boot
oder Häuschen auf einer der Inseln
besitzen, hat die Stiftung Stockholmer Schären das ,,Utö-Pro-
jekt'' eingerichtet. Auf der Insel
Utö stehen zur Verfügung: Hotel,
Ferienwohnungen, Dienstlei-
stungszentrum, Boot- und Fahr-
radvermietung.

Yachtsmen flock to the guest-harbour of
Utö and the convenient service centre. And
some rent bicycles to enjoy the lovely island.

Utös idyllischer Yachthafen, wo man auch
ein Fahrrad mieten kann, um das Inselinne-
re zu erforschen.

Sunday evening in Rindösund, Stockholmers on their way back to the city.

Sonntagabend im Rindösund – Stockholmer
auf dem Weg nach Hause.

Life in the archipelago—stark, beautiful.

Kargheit der Schären.

The archipelago steamers—often the only
link between the islands and the city.

Die weiße Flotte – oft die einzige Verbin-
dung zwischen den Schären und der Stadt.

Honour, Duty, Will are the famous words engraved on the tomb-stone of great Swedish hero Carl von Döbeln.

Ehre, Pflicht, Willen – Wahlspruch am Grabstein General von Döbelns, glückloser Held aus Schwedens letztem Krieg von 1809.

The Palace of Drottningholm outside Stockholm from the middle of the 1600's with its magnificent park in the French 18th century style.

Schloß Drottningholm bei Stockholm aus dem 17. Jahrhundert mit seinem Park im Stil von Versailles.

Berns, the largest show restaurant in Stockholm. Famous since the late 1800s Berns is known for its shows and guest-appearances.

Berns Salonger – Stockholms größtes Show-Restaurant, seit Ende des letzten Jahrhunderts Hochburg des Stockholmer Show-Geschäfts.

Gröna Lund, amusement park in Djurgården, opened first in august 1883 with one large attraction: The huge, horse-driven merry-go-round. Now a very modern and sophisticated carnival.

Gröna Lund – Stockholms Tivoli, das bei seiner Eröffnung im August 1883 nur eine einzige größere Attraktion aufwies, ein von Pferden gezogenes Karussell. Heute ein Vergnügungspark mit allen Schikanen.

8

The history of Stockholm

1252 Stockholm is founded. The name of Stockholm appears for the first time in writing, in two letters written by Birger Jarl.

1523 Entry of Gustav Vasa into Stockholm. Stockholm becomes the capital and administrative centre of the Vasa Kingdom.

1582 The population of Stockholm is estimated at 8,000 persons.

1618 The oarswomen known as *roddarmadamer* begin to operate Stockholm's local water traffic.

1618–1648 During the Thirty Years' War Sweden develops into a major power, and the state administration grows rapidly. Commerce also expands rapidly, and by the end of Sweden's period as a major power Stockholm has a population of 50,000.

1697 The mediæval palace of Stockholm burns down, and work starts on the present building. (Tessin's Royal Palace was to be completed in 1751.)

1731 Hired cabs appear as a means of transport.

1772–1792 Under Gustav III, Stockholm becomes the cultural centre of Sweden. The Old Opera House and the Palace of the Prince Royal are built.

1835 A horse omnibus line starts between Gustav Adolfs Torg and Djurgårdsbron.

1863 The Stockholm City Council is formed and the Stockholm County Council (which excludes the Borough of Stockholm) meets for the first time.

1869 Constitution of the Waxholm Steamship Company (WÅAB).

1871 Inauguration of Stockholm Central Station.

1880 The first tram is put into operation.

1881 Opening of the first public telephone network.

1885 Construction of the first Katarina Elevator.

1891 Opening of the Skansen Open-Air Museum, on Djurgården.

1892 The first electricity works.

1895 Sweden's first electrified train, on the Djursholm line.

1897 The first motor car appears on the streets of Stockholm.

1899 Sweden's first motor omnibus starts in regular traffic in Stockholm.

1900 The first Nobel festivities are held in Stockholm and the first motor taxi is put into operation.

1905 The Swedish Parliament meets for the first time in its new building on the island of Helgeandsholmen.

1912 The Olympic Games are opened in the newly inaugurated Stockholm Stadium.

1919 Opening of the Stockholm freeport.

1923 The inauguration of Stockholm City Hall.

1936 The inauguration of Bromma Airport.

1941 The first trolley bus is put into service.

1943 The St. Erik's Fair opens for the first time in Stockholm.

1944 The inauguration of Söder Hospital.

1950 The first underground line is put into operation.

1953 Stockholm celebrates its septicentenary, and Kungsträdgården is introduced as the City's central site of festivities.

1959 The inauguration of Hötorgscity (first part).

1961 Salvaging of the Wasa, a royal ship-of-the-line which had lain on the seabed in Stockholm Harbour since 1628, when it sank on its maiden voyage.

1962 Arlanda Airport is opened for regular traffic.

1967 Right-hand traffic is introduced throughout Sweden.

1970 Introduction of the one-chamber Parliament.

1971 The present Stockholm County Council is formed by the incorporation of the former County Borough of Stockholm.

1973 Death of King Gustaf VI Adolf. His successor and grandson Carl XVI Gustaf becomes the new King in the Royal Palace.

Population

Year	Stockholm	County of Stockholm, total
1750	60,018	152,100
1800	75,517	171,797
1850	93,070	207,713
1900	300,624	473,476
1950	744,143	1 101,017
1960	808,294	1 217,014
1965	787,182	1 382,000
1970	740,486	1 477,234
1975	665,202	1 493,546
1978	653,929	1 519,114

The arts and culture

A large number of theatres, cinemas, museums, libraries etc. are available in the region of Stockholm.
In 1977, Stockholm had 62 cinemas with a seating capacity of 28,800.

Theatre and concert performances etc. in Stockholm 1977/78

	Performances	Attendance
Royal Dramatic Theatre	1,140	293,500
Stockholm Municipal Theatre	1,474	300,600
Other theatres	1,699	663,400
Opera: Royal Opera and the Drottningholm Court Theatre	386	241,100

Cultural institutions

Number of visitors	1977
Museum	43,700
Millesgården (works by the sculptor Carl Milles)	122,000
Liljevalch's Art Gallery	137,900
Waldemarsudde (home of the "painter prince", Prince Eugen)	152,600
Stockholm City Hall	184,300
Wasa Exhibition	467,000
Gröna Lund Funfair	1 139,700
Skansen Open-Air Museum	1 746,880

Education

The 9-year primary comprehensive is compulsory for all children from the age of 7. The number of children continuing at the secondary-level comprehensive is indicated below.

	Stockholm	County of Stockholm, total
Secondary comprehensive, total	19,706	38,972
Of which 3-year and 4-year lines	9,682	18,861
2-year lines (vocational, or vocationally geared)	6,353	15,029
Special courses.	3,671	5,082

Facilities for higher education include Stockholm University, the Royal College of Technology, and the Stockholm School of Economics.

Students at universities and colleges of higher education, Autumn Term 1976

	Total
Stockholm University	24,063
Karolinska Institutet (Royal Caroline Institute)	3,623
Other colleges	11,388
of which Royal College of Technology	5,504
Stockholm School of Economics	1,280
Stockholm School of Social Work and Public Administration	1,886

9

Sports

In Stockholm and its surroundings there are

10 golf courses
30 outdoor swimming pools
19 indoor swimming pools, and
12,000 berths in marinas,

plus a very large number of sports halls, sports grounds, tennis courts and football pitches, the largest of these being the Råsunda Football Stadium, Sundbyberg. Artificial ice-rinks for ice-hockey and bandy are also available.
Trotting tracks exist at Solvalla and at Täby Racecourse.

The climate

Mean temperature in Stockholm compared with certain other capitals.

MEAN TEMPERATURES

	January		July	
	Centigrade	Fahrenheit	Centigrade	Fahrenheit
Stockholm	−3	26	+18	64
London	+5	41	+18	64
New York City	+1	34	+25	77
Madrid	+4	40	+24	75
Paris	+3	37	+19	66

15 industrial groups with their head offices in the County of Stockholm

	Turnover in SKr. Mill.	No. of employees
Axel Johnson group	14,800.0	28,000
Electrolux	12,022.8	75,570
Statsföretag	10,291.0	43,690
LM Ericsson	9,021.0	61,400
Skånska Cementgjuteriet	7,623.0	24,900
Beijerinvest	7,410.0	9.800
Slakteriförbundet	7,154.2	10,800
NK-Åhléns	7,127.9	20,950
SAS	7,049.7	21,680
Systembolaget	6,645.2	2,900
Svenska Tändsticks	5,354.0	23,250
Gränges	5,135.0	15,630
Alfa-Laval	4,986.3	17,760
Atlas Copco	4,742.3	17,660
Arla	4,545.0	5,620

These companies are among the 25 largest in Sweden.

Copyright: ©1979 K.W. Gullers

Text: Birgitta Juhlin-Dannfelt

Other photographers: Carl G. Dahlerus
Svante Hedin
Kjell Johansson
Sture Karlsson
Östen Matsson
Pål Nils Nilsson/TIO
Karl-Erik Sundqvist
Pressens Bildarkiv

Adaption: Exportspråk AB/English and German
Reproduction: Fägerblads Repro AB, Västerås, Sweden
Paper: Offblade 135 g, MoDo Papper AB, Sweden
Printing: AB Fälths Tryckeri, Värnamo, Sweden
Publisher: Gullers International ab

ISBN 91-85228-70-2

STOK

Orientem

ST

Templ. S. Mariæ

AUSTRALE

Templ. S. Gertrudis

MÄLCR LACVS